SINGLE SPIES

SINGLE SPIES

A double bill

by
ALAN BENNETT

faber and faber
LONDON · BOSTON

First published in 1989
by Faber and Faber Limited
3 Queen Square London WC1N 3AU

Photoset by Parker Typesetting Service Leicester
Printed in Great Britain by
Richard Clay Ltd Bungay Suffolk
All rights reserved

A CIP record for this book is available from the British Library

ISBN 0-571-14105-6

CONTENTS

Some years ago a stage play of mine, *The Old Country*, was running in the West End. The central character, Hilary, played by Alec Guinness, was a Foreign Office defector living in Russia. Hilary was generally identified as Philby, though that had not been my intention, the character having much more in common with a different sort of exile, W. H. Auden. However during the run of *The Old Country* friends and well-wishers would come round after the performance, often with reminiscences of Philby and his predecessors, Burgess and Maclean. One of these was Coral Browne who told me of her visit to Russia with the Shakespeare Memorial Theatre in 1958 and the particular incidents that make up *An Englishman Abroad*.

The picture of the elegant actress and the seedy exile sitting in a dingy Moscow flat through a long afternoon listening again and again to Jack Buchanan singing 'Who stole my heart away?' seemed to me funny and sad but it was a few years before I got round to writing it up. It was only when I sent Coral Browne the first draft of the television film that I found she had kept not merely Burgess's letters, thanking her for running his errands, but also her original notes of his measurements and even his cheque (uncashed and for £6) to treat her and one of her fellow actors to lunch at the Caprice. The original script of the television film was quite close to the version now presented on the stage. It had no exterior shots because I knew no BBC budget would run to filming in Moscow or some foreign substitute. I introduced the exteriors only when a suitable (and a suitably economic) substitute for Moscow was found in Dundee.

I have put some of my own sentiments into Burgess's mouth. 'I can say I love London. I can say I love England. I can't say I love my country, because I don't know what that means', is a fair statement of my own, and I imagine many people's position. The Falklands War helped me to understand how a fastidious stepping-aside from patriotism could be an element in characters as different as Blunt and Burgess. Certainly in the spy fever that followed the unmasking of Professor Blunt I felt more sympathy with the hunted than the hunters.

I never met Blunt, but though he seems to have been an altogether less likeable character than Burgess he is a more familiar type, at any rate in academic circles. Championed by his pupils he was less favourably regarded by some of his colleagues, who found him arrogant and opinionated. There are plenty of dons like this, in whom shyness, self-assurance and deep conviction combine to give an uncongenial impression. Housman and Wittgenstein are perhaps the most distinguished examples. In death such characters are invariably filed under the obituarist's catch-all 'Did not suffer fools gladly'.

In the first play it is suggested that Burgess was a spy because he wanted a place where he was alone, and that having a secret supplies this. I believe this to be psychologically true, but there is a sense too that an ironic attitude towards one's country and a scepticism about one's heritage is a part of that heritage. And so, by extension, is the decision to betray it. It is irony activated.

I find it hard to drum up any patriotic indignation over either Burgess or Blunt, or even Philby. No one has ever shown that Burgess did much harm, except to make fools of people in high places. Because he made jokes, scenes and, most of all, passes, the general consensus is that he was rather silly. Blunt was not silly and there have been attempts to show that his activities had more far-reaching consequences, but again he seems to be condemned as much out of pique and because he fooled the Establishment as for anything that he did. It is Philby who is always thought to be the most congenial figure. Clubbable, able to hold his liquor, a good man in a tight corner, he commends himself to his fellow journalists, who have given him a good press. But of all the Cambridge spies he is the only one of whom it can be proved without doubt that he handed over agents to torture and death.

It suits governments to make treachery the crime of crimes, but the world is smaller than it was and to conceal information can be as culpable as to betray it. As I write evidence is emerging of a nuclear accident at Windscale in 1957, the full extent of which was hidden from the public. Were the politicians and civil servants responsible for this less culpable than our Cambridge villains? Because for the spies it can at least be said that they were risking their own skins whereas the politicians were risking someone else's.

Of course Blunt and Burgess and co. had the advantage of us in that they still had illusions. They had somewhere to turn. The trouble with treachery nowadays is that if one does want to betray one's country there is no one satisfactory to betray it to. If there were, more people would be doing it.

AB

Single Spies, a double bill of *An Englishman Abroad* and *A Question of Attribution*, was first performed at the Royal National Theatre, London, on 1 December 1988. The cast was as follows:

An Englishman Abroad

CORAL	Prunella Scales
BURGESS	Simon Callow
TOLYA	Paul Brightwell
TAILOR	Alan Bennett
SHOP ASSISTANT	Edward Halsted
Director	Alan Bennett
Designer	Bruno Santini
Lighting	Paul Pyant

A Question of Attribution

BLUNT	Alan Bennett
RESTORER	David Terence
CHUBB	Simon Callow
PHILLIPS	Crispin Redman
COLIN	Brett Fancy
HMQ	Prunella Scales
Director	Simon Callow
Designer	Bruno Santini
Lighting	Paul Pyant
Music	Dominic Muldowney

AN ENGLISHMAN ABROAD

CHARACTERS

BURGESS

CORAL

TOLYA

TAILOR

SHOP ASSISTANT

A projection screen hides the set. Stage right of the screen is a bentwood chair. The screen glows red and projected on it is the head of Stalin as we hear a record of Jack Buchanan singing 'Who stole my heart away?'.

The song fades as CORAL BROWNE *enters stage right. She is a striking woman, tall and elegant, and carries a luxurious fur coat.*

CORAL: Stalin died in 1953. I was in *Affairs of State* at the time, a light comedy that had a decent run at the Cambridge. Stalin had had a decent run too, though I'd never been a fan of the old boy, even during the war when he was all the rage. It wasn't so much the cult of personality that put me off (being in the theatre I'm no stranger to that); it was the moustache. One smiles, but more judgements than people care to admit are grounded in such trivialities, and when you're just a fool of an actress like me you don't mind coming out with it.

After Uncle Joe's death they played with the understudies for a bit, then brought in a cast of unknowns in something called The Thaw. Soviet experts in the West (what nowadays would be called 'experienced Kremlin-watchers') thought that this show was going to run and run, predicting – poor loves – that the Iron Curtain was about to go up and stay up. Ah well. Incidentally, don't let any of this deceive you into thinking I took any sort of interest in Soviet affairs. Actresses are excused newspapers much as delicate boys used to be excused games; the only paper I see regularly is *The Stage*, and its coverage of the comings and goings in the Politburo is, to say the least, cursory.

Still, there were repercussions, even on me. When peace breaks out suddenly, as it did then, culture is first on the menu, actors and musicians sent in ahead of the statesmen like the infantry before the tanks. We had the Red Army Choir; they got the Stratford Memorial Theatre in *Hamlet*. Michael Redgrave was the eponymous prince, and notwithstanding I was scarcely five minutes older than he was, I played his mother.

(GUY BURGESS *enters stage left. He is in his early fifties, a man who has once been handsome but is now running to seed.*)

BURGESS: Hearing that Stalin had died one cheered up no end. It wasn't just that I was glad to see the back of the old bugger, though I was, but for the first time since I'd come to Moscow in 1951 I found I'd something to do. Death always means work for somebody, and one was suddenly very busy reading the papers, monitoring news broadcasts, collating and analysing Western reactions to the Marshal's somewhat overdue departure. However, in no time at all, they had him tucked in beside Lenin on Red Square, and life returned to what I had come to regard as normal – doing *The Times* crossword, the *Statesman* competition, reading Trollope and Jane Austen. A gentleman of leisure. Of course the most accomplished exiles are, and always have been, the Russians. They're tutors in it practically. So, in a sense we had come to the right place.

What made it harder to bear was that no one in what one couldn't help thinking of as the outside world actually knew we were here. For the first few years of our sojourn we were kept very much under wraps – no letters, no phone calls, nothing. It made Greta Garbo look gregarious. I say 'we', meaning my colleague Maclean, with some diffidence. It's dispiriting to find oneself yoked permanently to someone who was never meant to be more than a travelling companion (besides having been a fellow travelling companion, of course). Now it was 'we', handcuffed together in the same personal pronoun.

Quarantine or honeymoon, our period of probation ended when we were revealed to the world's press in Moscow in 1956. After that, though we never exactly hit the cocktail party circuit and still had to mind our ps and qs, there was less – shall we say – skulking. (BURGESS *exits left.*)

CORAL: Dissolve to my dressing-room in the Moscow Art Theatre one night after the performance. I am sitting there, applying the paint-stripper, when I hear a commotion next door.

Suddenly Hamlet bursts in. Someone is being sick in his dressing room, would I assist?

Now vomiting is not childbirth. If one is having a baby a helping hand is not unwelcome. If one is having a puke, one is best left alone to get on with it. Remembering always that nausea requires patience. One of the few lessons I have learned in life is that when one is sick it is always in threes. Judging by the state of the carpet this was a lesson this particular gentleman had yet to learn. When his face came out of the basin I found I knew it, though not by name. The moment for introductions was long since past and Redgrave did not make them. I cleaned the man up, noting that he was English, he was upper class, and he was drunk. It was only later that night when a note was slipped under my door at the hotel that I found out he was also Guy Burgess. (CORAL *has put on her fur coat and she takes a note from the pocket.*) 'Bring a tape measure.' Bring a tape measure?

(*The motif of Stalin has faded from the screen and as we hear* BURGESS *singing the screen rises to reveal his very untidy flat. There is an easy chair, a sofa and a small table, several bookshelves filled to overflowing with (English) books and papers and at the rear of the flat a kitchenette. Through an alcove is a double bed, unmade and the sheets unwashed and stage left is a pianola.*)

BURGESS: (*Singing off*)

Oh God our help in ages past
Our hope for years to come,
Our shelter from the stormy blast
And our eternal home.

(BURGESS *wanders in, shaving.*)

Before the hills in order stood
Or earth received her frame

(*The doorbell rings.*)

From everlasting Thou art God,
It's open.
Through endless years the same.

(BURGESS *hurriedly clears some dirty clothes from a chair and as an afterthought flings the heaped contents of an ashtray under the sofa, as* CORAL *enters through the hallway stage right.*)

BURGESS: (*To* CORAL) Hello.

CORAL: (*Puffed*) The stairs!

BURGESS: I know. I'm sorry. Recover. What a splendid coat. Let me take it. (*He buries his face in the grand fur coat before dropping it, pretty unceremoniously, on the sofa.*)

BURGESS: Mmm. Have a drink.

CORAL: Please.

BURGESS: I've just been tidying up. (*He sweeps some stuff to the floor and removes his soap and towel.*)

CORAL: One moment. My soap. This is my soap.

BURGESS: It is. It is. 'Palmolive – for that schoolgirl complexion.'

CORAL: So it was you who took my cigarettes?

BURGESS: One wasn't well. (*He hands her a glass, which she surreptitiously cleans on her skirt. He pours her a drink.*)

CORAL: My Scotch?

(BURGESS *smiles.*)

BURGESS: One should have asked.

CORAL: You even took my face powder.

BURGESS: I know. One is such a coward. Still. You came. I thought you'd chuck. (*He raises his glass in a toast.*)

CORAL: I nearly did. I seem to have trekked halfway across Moscow. Is there something in the Communist Manifesto against taxis? One never sees any. And that woman on the door downstairs!

BURGESS: I know. How did you get past her?

CORAL: I gave her my lipstick.

BURGESS: I can't think what she'll do with it. I'm always struck by her pronounced resemblance to the late Ernest Bevin. They could be sisters.

CORAL: Did you enjoy the play?

BURGESS: What play?

CORAL: Our play. *Hamlet.*

BURGESS: Loved it. Loved it. I liked the look of Laertes. He goes rather well into tights.

CORAL: That's what he thinks.

4

BURGESS: He looked as if he'd put a couple of King Edwards down there. That apart, of course, such a pleasure to hear the language so beautifully spoken.

CORAL: I was told you were asleep.

BURGESS: No. Though one did have a tiny zizz. After all, one has seen it before. Are there still a couple of music-hall comedians on the wireless called Nat Mills and Bobby?

CORAL: I don't know them.

BURGESS: Their catchphrase was, 'Well, why don't you get on with it?' I always feel they would have come in handy in *Hamlet*. Still. The comrades lapped it up. But they do, of course, culture. How do you like Moscow?

CORAL: Loathe it, darling. I cannot understand what those Three Sisters were on about. It gives the play a very sinister slant. (*She walks about the flat.*)

BURGESS: It's hardly luxury's lap, I'm afraid. A pigsty, in fact. I used to live in Jermyn Street. Tragic, you might think, but not really. That was a pigsty, too. By their standards it's quite commodious. Palatial even. One is very lucky.

CORAL: What is that smell?

BURGESS: Me probably.

CORAL: No. Besides that. If it's our lunch, it's burning.

BURGESS: Oh. Now. It might be. (*He gets up unhurriedly and goes into the kitchenette.*) Yes, it is. It was stew. (*He peers into the pan.*) One could salvage some of it? (*He shows it to* CORAL.)

CORAL: Hardly.

BURGESS: Perhaps not. (*He returns to the kitchen with it.*) However. All is not lost. I managed to scrounge two tomatoes this morning, and . . . quite a talking point . . . a grapefruit. Shall we perch? I generally do.
(*He draws* CORAL's *chair to the table and himself sits on the arm of the easy chair.*)

CORAL: (*Faintly*) Treats.
(*He puts a tomato on her plate and eats his like an apple.*)

BURGESS: Garlic?

CORAL: No, thank you.

BURGESS: I love it. (*He eats several cloves.*) Yum yum. Now. Tell me all the gossip. Do you see Harold Nicolson?

CORAL: I *have* seen him. I don't know him.

BURGESS: Oh, don't you? Nice man. Nice man. What about Cyril Connolly?

CORAL: I haven't run into him either.

BURGESS: Really? That must be quite difficult. He's everywhere. You know him, of course?

CORAL: As a matter of fact, no.

BURGESS: Oh. One somehow remembers everyone knowing everyone else. Everyone I knew knew everyone else. Auden – do you know him? Pope Hennessy?

CORAL: (*Manfully*) The theatre's in a terrible state.

BURGESS: Is it?

CORAL: Three plays closed on Shaftesbury Avenue in one week.

BURGESS: That's tragic. Some ballet on ice is coming here. The comrades are all agog. I'm rather old-fashioned about ice. I used to direct at Cambridge, you know. That's how I know your star, Mr Redgrave. I directed him in *Captain Brassbound's Conversion*. It was an average production, but notable for a memorable performance by Arthur Marshall as Lady Cicely Waynflete. Happy days. One thinks back and wonders, did one miss one's way. What would have happened had one gone into the theatre? Nothing, I suppose.

CORAL: Who knows, you might just have been Kenneth Tynan's cup of tea.

BURGESS: Oh, do you think so? Do you know him?

CORAL: Slightly.

BURGESS: He happened after we came away. You're not eating your tomato.

CORAL: I'm not hungry.

BURGESS: I am. (*He takes it.*) This garlic!

CORAL: Do you see many people here?

BURGESS: Oh yes. Heaps of chums. You don't know what you're missing with this tomato.

CORAL: There's your other half, I suppose.

BURGESS: What? Oh yes. He's taken up the balalaika. We play duets.

CORAL: Maclean?

BURGESS: No. Oh *no*. Not Maclean. (*He bursts out laughing*.) Taking up the balalaika! Maclean's not my friend. Oh, ducky. Oh no, not Maclean. He's so unfunny, no jokes, no jokes at all. Positively the last person one would have chosen if one had had the choice. And here we are on this terrible tandem together – Debenham and Freebody, Crosse and Blackwell, Auden and Isherwood, Burgess and Maclean. Do you know Auden?

CORAL: You asked me. No.

BURGESS: (*Going over to the kitchenette*) Sweet man. Don't look. The seeds get inside my plate. (*He swills his teeth*.) People ask me if I have any regrets. The one regret I have is that before I came away I didn't get kitted out with a good set of National Health gnashers. Admirable as most things are in the Soviet Socialist Republic, the making of dentures is still in its infancy. (*Pause*.) Actually, there's no one in Moscow at all. It's like staying up in Cambridge for the Long Vac. One makes do with whoever's around.

CORAL: Me.

BURGESS: No, no. And in any case I asked you here for a reason. Did you bring a tape measure?

CORAL: I did. (*She produces it*.)

BURGESS: Good. (BURGESS *puts on his jacket. His suit is well cut but shabby, the knees of the trousers darned and darned again*.) I want you to measure me for some suits. From my tailor. I only have one suit. It's the one I came away in and I've fallen down a lot since then.

CORAL: But I shan't know where to start. What measurements will he want?

BURGESS: Measure it all. He'll work it out. He's a nice man. (*He gets her pencil and paper. She draws the figure of a man on the paper*.)

CORAL: Won't your people here get you a suit?

BURGESS: What people?

CORAL: The authorities.

BURGESS: Oh yes, but have you seen them? Clothes have never

7

been the comrades' strong point. Besides, I don't want to look like everybody else, do I? (*He bends his arm for her to measure.*) I seem to remember doing this.

CORAL: Your arms can't have altered.

BURGESS: I never cared tuppence for clothes before . . . Measure me round here . . . I was kitted out in the traditional garb of my class. Black coat, striped trousers. Pinstripe suit and tweeds for weekends. Shit order, of course. Always in shit order. But charm, I always had charm.

CORAL: (*Measuring away*) You still have charm. She said through clenched teeth.

BURGESS: But not here. Not for them. For charm one needs words. I have no words. And, short of my clothes, no class. I am 'The Englishman'. 'Would you like to go to bed with the Englishman?' I say. Not particularly. One got so spoiled during the war. The joys of the black-out. London awash with rude soldiery. (*He says a Russian phrase.*) *Skolko zeem, skolko let.*

CORAL: What does that mean?

BURGESS: *Skolko zeem, skolko let?* It means the same as our '*Où sont les neiges d'antan?*' Nostalgia, you see, knows no frontiers.

CORAL: Do you speak Russian?

BURGESS: I manage. Maclean's learned it, naturally. Swot. I haven't. I ought to, simply for the sex. Boys are quite thin on the ground here. I can't speak their language and they can't speak mine, so when one does manage to get one it soon palls. Sex needs language.

(CORAL *is still busy measuring.*)

CORAL: At least you've found a friend.

BURGESS: Tolya? Yes. Except I'm not sure whether I've found him or been allotted him. I know what I've done to be given him. But what has he done to be given me? Am I a reward or a punishment? He plays the balalaika. I play the pianola. It's fun. He's an electrician with the ballet. Of course he may be a policeman. If he is a policeman he's a jolly good actor. Forster lived with a policeman, didn't he? You know him?

8

(CORAL *shakes her head*.)

Nice man. Getting on now, I suppose.

CORAL: I feel I'm somewhat of a disappointment in the friends department. I gather Paul Robeson is coming here. Now I know him.

BURGESS: Do you? He's a big favourite with the comrades. What with being black, and red. I remember when I was posted to the Washington Embassy the Secretary of State, dear old Hector McNeill, had me in his room and gave me a lecture about what I should and shouldn't do when I got there: I mustn't be too openly left-wing, mustn't get involved in the colour question, and above all I must avoid homosexual incidents. I said, 'To sum up, Hector, what you're saying is, "Don't make a pass at Paul Robeson".'

CORAL: I wouldn't either.

Nobody will believe me when I go home. 'What did you do in Moscow, darling?' 'Nothing much, I measured Guy Burgess's inside leg.'

BURGESS: I shouldn't think one's inside leg alters, do you? It's one of the immutables. 'The knee is such a distance from the main body, whereas the groin, as your honour knows, is upon the very curtain of the place.'

CORAL: Come again.

BURGESS: *Tristram Shandy*. Lovely book. Of course, you wouldn't do that.

CORAL: Do what?

BURGESS: Go round telling everybody. My people here wouldn't like that.

CORAL: (*Looking up from her knees*) No?

BURGESS: No. A hat would be nice. I've written down the name of my hatters. And my bootmaker.

CORAL: It's a trousseau.

BURGESS: Yes. For a shotgun marriage.

CORAL: How do you know he won't say no, your tailor?

BURGESS: Why should he say no? It would be vulgar to say no.

CORAL: Well, I'll see what I can do.

(*She prepares to go.* BURGESS *doesn't make any move.*)

BURGESS: Don't go yet. I don't want you to go yet. You mustn't go yet.

CORAL: Can't we go somewhere? You could show me the sights.

BURGESS: In due course. But we can't go yet. I have to wait for a telephone call. When the telephone call comes I'm permitted to leave.

CORAL: Who from?

BURGESS: Oh . . . you know . . . my people. It's generally around four.

CORAL: That's another two hours.

BURGESS: Yes. 'What then is to be done?' as Vladimir Ilyitch almost said. I know. I can play you my record.
(*He puts a record on the gramophone. It is Jack Buchanan singing 'Who stole my heart away?'. They listen to this in its entirety.*)
Good, isn't it? It's Jack Buchanan.

CORAL: Yes.

BURGESS: Is he still going?

CORAL: Yes.

BURGESS: Did you ever come across him?

CORAL: Yes. I did actually. We nearly got married.

BURGESS: And?

CORAL: He jilted me.

BURGESS: Oh. Small world. Still. It's a good record. (*He puts it on again.*)

CORAL: And so we sat there in that dreary flat all through that long afternoon waiting for the telephone to ring. From time to time he played his record and I had to listen to my ex-beau. I was puzzled as to how he had managed to get all his books there.

BURGESS: Someone sent them. A well-wisher. The desk belonged to Stendhal.

CORAL: Did you have that in London?

BURGESS: Yes.

CORAL: Couldn't the same person who sent you your books get you the suits?

BURGESS: No.

CORAL: No?

BURGESS: No.

CORAL: When I came into the flats I noticed a boy sitting on the stairs playing chess.

BURGESS: Police. When I first came I used to be shadowed by rather grand policemen. That was when I was a celebrity. Nowadays they just send the trainees. I wish I could lead them a dance. But I can't think of a dance to lead them.

Mind you, they're more conscientious than their English counterparts. All that last week before we left we were tailed. Maclean lived in Sussex so on the Friday evening we went to Waterloo, dutifully followed by these two men in raincoats. They saw us as far as the barrier and then went home. On the very civilized principle, I suppose, that nothing happens at the weekend. It was the only reason we got away. (*Pause.*) Waterloo the same, is it?

CORAL: Yes. (*Pause.*) What do you miss most?

BURGESS: Apart from the Reform Club, the streets of London, and occasionally the English countryside, the only thing I truly miss is gossip. The comrades, though splendid in every other respect, don't gossip in quite the way we do or about quite the same subjects.

CORAL: Pardon me for saying so, dear, but the comrades seem to me a sad disappointment in every department. There's no gossip, their clothes are terrible and they can't make false teeth. What else is there?

BURGESS: (*Gently*) The system. Only, being English, you wouldn't be interested in that. (*Pause.*) My trouble is, I lack what the English call character. By which they mean the power to refrain. Appetite. The English never like that, do they? Unconcealed appetite. For success. Women. Money. Justice. Appetite makes them uncomfortable. What do people say about me in England?

CORAL: They don't much any more.

(*She gets up and starts tidying the room. Folding clothes, washing dishes.* BURGESS *watches.*)

I thought of you as a bit like Oscar Wilde.
(BURGESS *laughs*.)
BURGESS: No, no. Though he was a performer. And I was a performer. Both vain. But I never pretended. If I wore a mask it was to be exactly what I seemed. And I made no bones about politics. My analyses of situations, the précis I had to submit at the Foreign Office, were always Marxist. Openly so. Impeccably so. Nobody minded. 'It's only Guy.' 'Dear old Guy.' Quite safe. If you don't wish to conform in one thing, you should conform in all the others. And in all the important things I did conform. 'How can he be a spy? He goes to my tailor.' The average Englishman, you see, is not interested in ideas. You can say what you like about political theory and no one will listen. You could shove a slice of the Communist Manifesto in the Queen's Speech and no one would turn a hair. Least of all, I suspect, HMQ. Am I boring you?
CORAL: It doesn't matter. (*She investigates the bookshelves. Takes a book out. Puts it back.*)
BURGESS: I'll think of a hundred and one things to ask you when you've gone. How is Cyril Connolly?
CORAL: You've asked me that. I don't know.
BURGESS: You won't have come across Anthony Blunt then?
CORAL: No. Isn't he quite grand?
BURGESS: Very grand. That's art. Art is grand. Art and opera. It's the way to get on.
CORAL: Is he nice?
BURGESS: Not particularly. Though nice is what you generally have to be, isn't it? 'Is he nice?' So little, England. Little music. Little art. Timid, tasteful, nice. But one loves it. Loves it. You see, I can say I love London. I can say I love England. But I can't say I love my country. I don't know what that means. Do you watch cricket?
CORAL: No. Anyway, it's changed.
BURGESS: Cricket?
CORAL: London.
BURGESS: Why? I don't want it to change. Why does anybody

want to change it? They've no business changing it. The fools. You should stop them changing it. Band together.

CORAL: Listen, darling. I'm only an actress. Not a bright lady, by your standards. I've never taken much interest in politics. If this is communism I don't like it because it's dull. And the poor dears look so tired. But then Australia is dull and that's not communism. And look at Leeds. Only it occurs to me that we have sat here all afternoon pretending that spying, which is what you did, darling, was just a minor social misdemeanour, no worse – and I'm sure in certain people's minds much better – than being caught in a public lavatory the way gentlemen in my profession constantly are, and that it's just something one shouldn't mention. Out of politeness. So that we won't be embarrassed. That's very English. We will pretend it hasn't happened because we are both civilized people.

Well, I'm not English. And I'm not civilized. I'm Australian. I can't muster much morality, and outside Shakespeare the word treason to me means nothing. Only, you pissed in our soup and we drank it. Very good. Doesn't affect me, darling. And I will order your suit and your hat. And keep it under mine. Mum. Not a word. But for one reason and one reason only: because I'm sorry for you. Now in your book . . . in your *real* book . . . that probably adds my name to the list of all the other fools you've conned. But you're not conning me, darling. Pipe isn't fooling pussy. I *know*.

(*The telephone rings.*)

BURGESS: Pity. I was enjoying that. (*He picks up the phone.*) You spoiled the lady's big speech. *Da. Da. Spassibo.* (*He puts the phone down.*) Finished?

CORAL: I just want to be told why.

BURGESS: It seemed the right thing to do at the time. And solitude, I suppose.

CORAL: Solitude?

BURGESS: If you have a secret you're alone.

CORAL: But you told people. You told several people.

BURGESS: No point in having a secret if you make a secret of it.
Actually the other thing you might get me is an Etonian tie.
This one's on its last legs.
(*They have got up ready to go when* TOLYA, *a young Russian,*
comes in.)
Ah, here's Tolya.
(*He kisses him.*)
Tolya. This is Miss Browne. She is an actress. From
England.

TOLYA: (*Pronouncing it very carefully*) How do you do? How are
you?

BURGESS: Very good. If you give him an English cigarette he'll be
your friend for life.
(CORAL *does so.* TOLYA *takes a cigarette but is then fascinated*
by the packet and takes that also. He examines it carefully then
hands it back.)

CORAL: No, please. Feel free.
(CORAL *lights his cigarette with her lighter.*)

TOLYA: Thank you.
(*But now her lighter has caught his eye and he takes that too,*
flicking it on and off, fascinated.)

TOLYA: *Chudyessna!*

BURGESS: Oh dear. Sorry.
(*Reluctantly* TOLYA *offers the lighter back.*)

CORAL: (*Resigned*) No, please.

BURGESS: (*Taking the lighter and handing it back to* CORAL)
No, you mustn't. He'll take anything. He's a real Queen
Mary. But you . . . wouldn't be able to order him a suit,
would you? Off the peg. He'd look so nice.

CORAL: (*Desperately*) Anything. Anything.

TOLYA: (*In Russian*) *Ya hotyel bwi eegrat dlya nyeyo.*

BURGESS: *Da? Samnoy?*

TOLYA: *Konyeshna.*

BURGESS: Tolya wants us to play you a tune. Let him. He'd be so
pleased. Just five minutes.
(*They embark on the duet 'Take a pair of sparkling eyes' from*
Gilbert and Sullivan's The Gondoliers. BURGESS *shouts above*

the music.)

What do you think? Reward or punishment?

(*The music continues as the lights fade, hiding the room.*)

CORAL: When we left the flat he took me to a church not far from where he lived. I've since been told that it was kept open just to indicate that there still were such places. The singing was very good. Apparently it was where the opera singers went to warm up for the evening's performance.

As a rule I don't have much time for men's tears. It's like blowing smoke rings, crying is a facility some men have. And it wasn't as if there was anything particularly English about the service. It wasn't like church or school, and yet when I looked at him the tears were rolling down his cheeks. He left me outside my hotel.

(CORAL *goes stage right, leaving* BURGESS *in the spot, stage left.*)

BURGESS: Something else you could do for me when you get back. Ring the old mum. Tell her I'm all right. Looking after myself. She's been here once. Loved it. Too frail now. I would come back to see her but apparently it's not on. Still got to stand in the corner, I suppose.

'Let him never come back to us.

There would be doubt, hesitation and pain.

Forced praise on our part, the glimmer of twilight,

Never glad confident morning again.'

Good old Browning. Goodbye. *Dosvidanya.*

(*The light fades on* BURGESS *as* CORAL *comes on, right, in a different coat and hat. A* TAILOR *enters, left, wearing a tape measure and carrying a swatch of samples.*)

CORAL: I'd like to order some suits.

TAILOR: Certainly madam.

CORAL: You've made suits for the gentleman before, but he now lives abroad.

TAILOR: I see.

(CORAL *hands him her bit of paper.*)

CORAL: I took his measurements. I'm not sure they're the right ones.

(*The* TAILOR *looks at the paper.*)

TAILOR: Oh yes. These are more than adequate. Could one know the gentleman's name?

CORAL: Yes. Mr Burgess.

TAILOR: We have two Mr Burgesses. I take this to be Mr Burgess G. How is Mr Burgess? Fatter, I see. One of our more colourful customers. Too little colour in our drab lives these days. Knowing Mr Guy he'll want a pinstripe. But a durable fabric. His suits were meant to take a good deal of punishment. I hope they have stood him in good stead.

CORAL: Yes. They have indeed.

TAILOR: I'm glad to hear it. Always getting into scrapes, Mr Guy. And your name is . . .?

CORAL: Browne.

TAILOR: There is no need for discretion here, madam.

CORAL: Truly.

TAILOR: My apologies. (*He looks at her in recognition.*) Of course. And this is the address. I see. We put a little of ourselves into our suits. That is our loyalty.

CORAL: And mum's the word.

TAILOR: Oh, madam. Mum is always the word here. Moscow or Maidenhead, mum is always the word.

(*The* TAILOR *exits left leaving* CORAL *in the spot right.*)

CORAL: And so it was with all the shops I went into, scarcely an eyebrow raised. When the parcels arrived he wrote to me, the letter dated 11 April 1958, Easter Sunday, to which he adds, 'a very suitable day to be writing to you, since I also was born on it, to the later horror of the Establishment of the country concerned'.

(BURGESS, *left, now takes over the letter.*)

BURGESS: I really find it hard to know how to thank you properly. Everything *fits*. No need for any alterations at all. Thank you. Thank you. In spite of your suggestion – invitation, to visit your friend Paul Robeson, I find myself too shy to call on him. Not so much shy as frightened. The *agonies* I remember on first meeting with people I really admire, E. M. Forster (and Picasso and Winston Churchill).

H. G. Wells was quite different, but one could get drunk
with him and listen to stories of his sex life. Fascinating.
How frightened one would be of Charlie Chaplin.

One more thing. What I really need, the only thing more,
is pyjamas. Russian ones can't be slept in, are not in fact
made for the purpose. What I would like if you can find it is
four pairs of white or off-white pyjamas . . .

(*A* SHOP ASSISTANT *brings on a chair, right.*)

ASSISTANT: If you could take a seat, madam, I'll just check.

CORAL: '. . . *Four* pairs. Quite plain and only those two colours.
Then at last my outfit will be complete and I shall look like a
real agent again.' (*She looks twice.*) 'Then I shall look like a
real gent again.'

(*The* SHOP ASSISTANT *returns.*)

ASSISTANT: I'm afraid, madam, that the gentleman in question
no longer has an account with us. His account was closed.

CORAL: I know. He wishes to open it again.

ASSISTANT: I'm afraid that's not possible.

CORAL: Why?

ASSISTANT: Well . . . we supply pyjamas to the Royal Family.

CORAL: So?

ASSISTANT: The gentleman is a traitor, madam.

CORAL: So? Must traitors sleep in the buff?

ASSISTANT: I'm sorry. We have to draw the line somewhere.

CORAL: So why here? Say someone commits adultery in your
precious nightwear. I imagine it has occurred. What happens
when he comes in to order his next pair of jim-jams. Is it
sorry, no can do?

ASSISTANT: I'm very sorry.

CORAL: (*Her Australian accent gets now more pronounced as she gets
crosser*) You keep saying you're sorry, dear. You were quite
happy to satisfy this client when he was one of the most
notorious buggers in London and a drunkard into the
bargain. Only then he was in the Foreign Office. 'Red piping
on the sleeve, Mr Burgess – but of course.' 'A discreet
monogram on the pocket, Mr Burgess?' Certainly. And
perhaps if you'd be gracious enough to lower your trousers,

Mr Burgess, we could be privileged enough to thrust our tongue between the cheeks of your arse. But not any more. Oh no. Because the gentleman in question has shown himself to have some principles, principles which aren't yours and, as a matter of interest, aren't mine. But that's it, as far as you're concerned. No more jamas for him. I tell you, it's pricks like you that make me understand why he went. Thank Christ I'm not English.

ASSISTANT: As a matter of fact, madam, our firm isn't English either.

CORAL: Oh? What is it?

ASSISTANT: Hungarian. (*He exits right.*)

CORAL: Oh, I said, and thinking of the tanks going into Budapest a year or two before, wished I hadn't made such a fuss. So I went down the street to Simpsons and got him some pyjamas there. Guy wrote to thank me and sent me a cheque for £6 to treat myself to supper at the Caprice. Which one could, of course, in those days. In those days. Anyway, that was the last I heard of him. He never did come back, of course, dying in 1963. Heart attack.

This comedy I was in at the Cambridge, *Affairs of State* – I played the wife of an elderly statesman. 'Your friends were great men in their time,' I had to say, 'only those who've managed to stay alive can now hardly manage to stay awake.' And that, of course, would have been the solution for Burgess, to live on to a great age. Had he been living now he would have been welcomed back with open arms, just as Mosley was a few years back. He could have written his memoirs, gone on all the chat shows, done *Desert Island Discs* . . . played his Jack Buchanan record again. In England, you see, age wipes the slate clean. (*She gets up.*) If you live to be ninety in England and can still eat a boiled egg they think you deserve the Nobel Prize.

(*Now smartly suited, wearing an overcoat and Homburg hat and carrying an umbrella* BURGESS *stands in the spot stage left, the picture of an upper-class Englishman. Accompanied as if on the pianola he starts to sing 'For he is an Englishman' from Gilbert and Sullivan's* HMS *Pinafore.*)

BURGESS: For he might have been a Roosian,
  A French or Turk or Proosian,
  Or perhaps I-tal-ian.
  For in spite of all temptations
  To belong to other nations,
  He remains an Englishman,
  He remains an Englishman.

(*As* BURGESS *sings he is drowned out by the full chorus and orchestra in a rousing climax, but before the music stops the light has faded on* BURGESS *and the screen drops in, bright and blank and* CORAL *stands in front of it as though after a film screening.*)

CORAL: At supper one night, after a showing of the film of this story in 1983, I met Lord Harlech, who as David Omsby-Gore had been Minister of State at the Foreign Office at the time Burgess was wanting to come back and see his mother. The Foreign Office and the security services were in a blue funk apparently. All the threats of prosecution that were conveyed to Burgess were pure bluff. Harlech said there was nothing it would have been safe to charge him with. Egg on too many faces, I suppose.

 'And what about the others?' I said. 'What others?' he said. I said I'd heard there were others. Still. But he just smiled.

A QUESTION OF ATTRIBUTION

*An inquiry
in which the circumstances are imaginary
but the pictures are real.*

A NOTE ON THE PAINTINGS

A Question of Attribution is concerned with two paintings, Titian's *Allegory of Prudence* in the National Gallery and the *Triple Portrait*, formerly attributed to Titian, which is in the collection of HM The Queen. The play owes a great deal to two articles in which these paintings are discussed, 'Titian's *Allegory of Prudence*' by Erwin Panofsky (in *Meaning in the Visual Arts*, Peregrine, 1974) and 'Five Portraits' by St John Gore (*Burlington Magazine*, vol. 100, 1958).

For understandable reasons we were not permitted to reproduce the actual *Triple Portrait* or its X-ray here or for the stage production. Fortunately there was a copy of it at Hardwick Hall, though this copy only included the original two figures. The 'third man', revealed when the royal picture was cleaned, was not in the Hardwick Hall version, which must therefore have been copied after he had been painted out. For the stage production we reproduced the Hardwick Hall paintings by courtesy of the National Trust, and the 'third man' was added to the picture by the graphics department at the National Theatre. This is the figure reproduced here, and though its shortcomings make the comparison with Titian's son, Orazio Vecelli, less than convincing, should anyone be interested enough to compare the two from the actual paintings they would, I think, find that the identification is certainly arguable.

At the moment, however, such a comparison would be difficult to make as the *Triple Portrait* cannot be seen. It used to hang at Hampton Court but since the 1986 fire it has not been on public view. Indeed, I have not seen it myself, knowing it only from the photographs which illustrate Mr St John Gore's article. There is a certain appropriateness about this, though, as one of the criticisms made of Anthony Blunt as an art historian was that he preferred to work from photographs rather than the real thing.

FIGURE I   *Titian and a Venetian Senator* (the *Triple Portrait*
before cleaning), taken from a slide used in the National Theatre
production.

FIGURE 2   The *Triple Portrait* (Figure 1 after cleaning), taken
from a slide used in the National Theatre production.

FIGURE 3 *Allegory of Prudence*, copyright the National Gallery.

26

FIGURE 4   A composite of the *Triple Portrait* and *Allegory of Prudence*, taken from a slide used in the National Theatre production.

CHARACTERS

BLUNT

CHUBB

PHILLIPS

HMQ

COLIN

RESTORER

ANTHONY BLUNT'S *room at the Courtauld Institute where he is the Director. The time is the late 1960s. There is a large eighteenth-century double door and a fine ormolu mounted table serving as a desk but in all other respects the room is a functioning office, the bookshelves crowded with reference books and with piles of octavo volumes on the floor. Above the desk and upstage of it is a projection screen with a slide projector on a nearby side-table.*

BLUNT *stands left of the screen and the* RESTORER, *a humbler figure in a dustcoat, to the right. Their positions resemble those of saints or patrons on either side of an altarpiece and some effort should be made in the production to create stage pictures which echo in this way the composition and lighting of old masters.*

BLUNT: Next.

> (*On the screen a slide of the* Triple Portrait *before cleaning (Figure 1).*)

RESTORER: More of the same, I'm afraid. It's an ex-Titian. Now thought to be by several hands.

BLUNT: Called?

> (*The* RESTORER *consults a catalogue or printed sheet.*)

RESTORER: *Titian and a Venetian Senator.*

BLUNT: And this is Titian on the left. He's not by Titian, certainly.

RESTORER: No. He's a copy of the Berlin self-portrait.

BLUNT: I don't know about the other gentleman.

RESTORER: He's been identified as the Chancellor of Venice, Andrea Franceschi.

> (*Pause.*)

BLUNT: I should warn you. I don't have an eye. K. Clark was saying the other day (I don't *think* the remark was directed at me) that people who look at Old Masters fall into three groups: those who see what it is without being told; those who see it when you tell them; and those who can't see it whatever you do. I just about make the second category. It means I can't date pictures. Made a terrible hash of the early

Poussins. Couldn't tell which came first. For an art historian it's rather humiliating. Like being a wine taster and having no sense of smell. (*Pause.*) People find me cold. I don't gush, I suppose.

RESTORER: Not much to gush about, this lot. Mind you, wait till you see Holyrood.

BLUNT: I'm not saying painting doesn't affect me. Ravished, sometimes. Well, what do we do? Give it a scrub?

RESTORER: Couldn't do any harm.

BLUNT: On. On.

(*A slide of a painting of St Lawrence being roasted over a grid comes up on the screen.*)

What frightful thing is happening here?

RESTORER: *The Martyrdom of St Lawrence.*

(BLUNT *groans.*)

BLUNT: Art!

(BLUNT *steps from the office set to a podium or lectern, stage left, and we should have a sense that he is in the middle of a lecture. The lecture is illustrated by slides projected on the screen; these slides include Giovanni Bellini's* Agony in the Garden, *an* Annunciation *and other appropriate images, details and martyrdoms.*)

Were we not inured to its imagery, however, it would seem a curious world, this world of Renaissance art; a place of incongruous punishments, where heads come on plates and skulls sport cleavers, and an angel, tremulous as a butterfly, waits patiently for the attention of a young girl who is pretending to read.

Doomed to various slow and ingenious extinctions the saints brandish the emblems of their suffering, the cross, the gridiron and the wheel, and submit to their fate readily and without fuss, howling agonies gone through without a murmur, the only palliative a vision of God and the assurance of Heaven. Remote though all this is from our sensibility, there is a sense in which one might feel that it is all very British. For flayed, dismembered, spitted, roasted, these martyrs seldom lose a drop of their *sang-froid*, so cool

about their bizarre torments the real emblems of their
martyrdom a silk dressing-gown and a long cigarette-holder;
all of them doing their far, far better thing in a dignified silence.
About suffering they were always wrong, the Old Masters.
(*Slide*.) In Bellini's *Agony in the Garden*, for instance, the
apostles, oblivious to all considerations but those of
perspective, are fast asleep on ground as brown and bare as an
end-of-the-season goalmouth, this sleep signifying indifference.

Above them on a rocky promontory of convenient
geology, Jesus kneels in prayer, an exercise that still goes on
in some places, though with less agony and less certainty of
address, this praying of less interest to the budding art
historian or to the social historian or even to someone who
has just wandered into the gallery out of the rain (and it is
salutary to remind ourselves, here at the Courtauld Institute,
that that is what art is for most people) . . . this praying, as I
say, of less interest to them than the reaper on the edge of a
field in a Breughel, say, who has his hand up a woman's
dress, another exercise that still goes on in most places,
though with no agony but the same certainty of address.
Here is threshing, which we now do mechanically. Here is
sex, which we do mechanically also. And here is crucifixion,
which we do not do. Or do differently. Or do indifferently. It
is a world in which time means nothing, the present overlaps
the future, and did the saint but turn his head he would see
his own martyrdom through the window.

(BLUNT *turns and on the other side of the stage, right, we see the
double doors open to reveal a man in a trilby and raincoat
carrying a briefcase. This is* CHUBB.)

Judas takes the pieces of silver in the Temple at the same
moment as in the next field he hangs himself. Christ begs
God in the garden to free him from a fate that is already
happening higher up the hill.

(*As the lectern or podium disappears* BLUNT *steps back into the
office where* CHUBB *is waiting.* CHUBB *is seemingly vague,
seemingly amiable. Socially he is not in the same class as*
BLUNT, *who is sophisticated and metropolitan;* CHUBB, *while*

not naïve, is definitely suburban. The slides on the screen have changed to photographs of various young men, taken singly or enlarged from group photographs of colleges and teams; all date from the thirties and are in black and white. Following each denial by BLUNT *a new photograph comes up on the screen.*)

BLUNT: No. No. N . . . no.

CHUBB: Sure?

BLUNT: It's the neck. The *neck* could be Piero della Francesca.

CHUBB: Who's he?

BLUNT: Well, he was many things, but he wasn't a member of the Communist Party. (*Pause.*) And in answer to your earlier question, the larger question, I would only say . . . again . . . it seemed the right thing to do at the time.

CHUBB: One more?

BLUNT: Do I have a choice?

(CHUBB *switches off the screen.*)

CHUBB: You're probably tired.

BLUNT: Not particularly.

CHUBB: All these functions.

BLUNT: I don't go to what you call 'functions'.

CHUBB: If you're in charge of the Queen's pictures you must often have to be in attendance.

BLUNT: Yes. On the pictures.

CHUBB: I'm disappointed. Don't you see the Queen?

BLUNT: The Crown is a large organization. To ask me if I see the Queen is like asking a shopgirl if she sees Swan or Edgar.

CHUBB: My wife saw her the other day. When she was visiting Surrey.

BLUNT: Your wife?

CHUBB: The Queen. She was up at six o'clock and secured an excellent vantage point outside Bentall's. Her Majesty was heard to say 'What a splendid shopping centre'. I wonder what she's really like.

BLUNT: Look her up. You must have a file on her.

CHUBB: Yes, we probably do. I meant, to chat to. Hob-nob with. As a person. You can't, of course, say. I appreciate that.

BLUNT: Why can't I say?

CHUBB: Royal servants can't, can they? Keeping mum is part of the job. It's like the Official Secrets Act. (*Pause.*) I'm sorry. That was unkind. More snaps?

(BLUNT *says nothing.*)

Some people do this for pleasure, you know. Holidays. Trips abroad. 'This is a delightful couple we ran into on the boat. He's in the Foreign Office and he's a lorry driver.' You must often get asked round to watch people's slides.

BLUNT: Never.

CHUBB: You don't live in Purley.

BLUNT: No.

(CHUBB *switches on the screen with another photograph.*)

How many more times. There is no one else that I know.

CHUBB: This morning I got up, cup of tea, read the *Telegraph*, the usual routine. Nothing on the agenda for today, I thought, why not toddle up to town and wander round the British Museum, sure to come across something of interest. Just turning into Great Russell Street when I remember there is something on the agenda. Your good self! What's more, I'm due at the Courtauld Institute in five minutes. So I about turn and head for Portman Square.

(*Pause.*)

BLUNT: And? I was under the impression this narrative was leading somewhere.

CHUBB: The point is, we sometimes know things we don't know. A bit of me, you see, must have known that I was coming here. (*He switches the screen off.*) Have you ever caught Her Majesty in an unguarded moment?

BLUNT: I thought it was my unguarded moments you were interested in.

CHUBB: It's just a titbit for my wife.

BLUNT: My function here is not to provide your wife with fodder for the hairdresser's.

CHUBB: She thinks my job is so dull.

BLUNT: And mine?

CHUBB: I'm sure you have colleagues who'd be delighted to be in your shoes.

33

BLUNT: Really? Having to see you all the time?

CHUBB: Oh. I was under the impression you enjoyed these little get-togethers. I always do.

BLUNT: You nearly forgot.

CHUBB: I forgot it was *today*. I thought you looked forward to these little chats. I thought it helped you relax. 'All the time.' It's only once a month. I now feel I'm a burden. (*Pause.*) We could always scrap them. It's true we don't seem to be getting anywhere.

BLUNT: I wouldn't want that.

CHUBB: You've only to say the word. I don't know, I must have got hold of the wrong end of the stick. I thought this was the way you wanted it.

BLUNT: It is. It is.

CHUBB: The alternative isn't ruled out. If you feel that . . .

BLUNT: I don't feel that at all. I . . . I had a late night.

CHUBB: You *were* at the Palace!

BLUNT: Initially, yes.

CHUBB: I knew you were. My wife saw your name in the paper. Well, I'm not surprised you're tired. You must always be on tenterhooks, frightened to put a foot wrong, having to watch every word. You must find it a terrible strain.

BLUNT: This?

CHUBB: *No*. Talking to the Queen. What is she really like?

BLUNT: Should we look at some more photographs?

CHUBB: In a moment. I'm upset that you find our talks wearisome.

BLUNT: I don't. I don't. It was an unforgivable remark. And not the case. On the whole I find them . . . stimulating.

CHUBB: Do you? Now truthfully.

BLUNT: They keep me on my toes.

CHUBB: I'm glad. Are you liked, by the way?

BLUNT: By whom?

CHUBB: I don't know. It occurs to me that you work rather hard at being a cold fish.

BLUNT: My pupils like me. My colleagues . . . I don't know. I have a life, you see. Two lives. Some of my colleagues scarcely have one.

CHUBB: They don't know about your other life.

BLUNT: In the Household.

CHUBB: I see. In that case, three lives. But who's counting. (*He laughs. Suddenly switches on the screen with a new photograph.*) You don't know this boy? Not a boy now, of course. Might have a beard.

BLUNT: Should I? Who is he?

CHUBB: Nobody.

(*The next photograph is of a guardsman in uniform.*)

BLUNT: No.

(*The same guardsman now naked.*)

CHUBB: Goodness gracious. How did that get here? Dear me. Just think if one of your students knocked at the door. Two gentleman looking at a picture of a naked guardsman. What would they think?

BLUNT: They might think it was Art. Or they might think it was two gentlemen looking at a picture of a naked guardsman. They would be profoundly unstartled by either.

(CHUBB *switches off the screen.*)

CHUBB: Do you ever go to the National Gallery?

BLUNT: One has to from time to time. Though I avoid opening hours. The public make it so intolerable.

CHUBB: I went in the other day.

BLUNT: Really?

CHUBB: First time in yonks.

BLUNT: Good.

CHUBB: No, not good. Not good at all. Better off sticking to museums. Museums I know where I am. An art gallery, I always come out feeling restless and dissatisfied. Troubled.

BLUNT: Oh dear.

CHUBB: In a museum I'm informed, instructed. But with art . . . I don't know. Is it that I don't get anything out of the pictures? Or the pictures don't get anything out of me? What am I supposed to think? What am I supposed to feel?

BLUNT: What do you feel?

CHUBB: Baffled. And also knackered. I ended up on a banquette looking at the painting that happened to be opposite and I thought, well, at least I can try and take this one in. But no. Mind you, I hate shopping. I suppose for you an art gallery is home from home.

BLUNT: Some more than others. Home is hardly the word for the Hayward.

CHUBB: But you'll know, for instance, what order they all come in, the paintings?

BLUNT: Well . . . Yes . . . one does . . . quite early on . . . acquire a sense of the sequence, the chronology of art. Shouldn't we be getting on?

CHUBB: You see, I don't have that. I've no map. And yet I know there's a whole world there.

BLUNT: Yes.

CHUBB: I'm determined to crack it. I'm like that. A year ago I couldn't have changed a fuse. Started going down to the library, the odd evening class: I've just rewired the whole house. What I thought I'd do with this was start at the beginning before artists had really got the hang of it . . . perspective, for instance, a person and a house the same size (I can't understand how they couldn't just see). And then I'm planning to follow it through until the Renaissance when the penny begins to drop and they start painting what is actually – you know – *there*. How does that strike you as an approach? It's not too sophisticated?

BLUNT: No. One couldn't honestly say that. It incorporates one or two misconceptions, which it would not at this stage be very useful to go into. Mustn't run before we can walk.

CHUBB: Tell me. I don't want to get off on the wrong foot.

BLUNT: Shouldn't we be looking at more photographs?

CHUBB: In a minute. The chronological approach is a mistake?

BLUNT: Not in itself. But art has no goal. It evolves but it does not necessarily progress. Just as the history of politics isn't simply a progress towards parliamentary democracy, so the history of painting isn't simply a progress towards photographic realism. Different periods have different styles, different ways of seeing the world. And what about the Impressionists or Matisse or Picasso?

CHUBB: Oh, I think they could do it properly if they wanted to. They just got bored.

(BLUNT *is exasperated.*)

That's the way art galleries are arranged. Crude beginnings, growing accomplishment, mastery of all the techniques . . . then to hell with the rules, let's kick it around a bit.

BLUNT: But why should a plausible illusion of nature be the standard? Do we say Giotto isn't a patch on Michelangelo because his figures are less lifelike?

CHUBB: Michelangelo? I don't think they are all that lifelike, frankly. The women aren't. They're just like men with tits, and the tits look as if they've been put on with an ice-cream scoop. Has nobody pointed that out?

BLUNT: Not in quite those terms.

(*Pause.*)

CHUBB: Are you sure your students like you?

BLUNT: Discussion is seldom at this level.

CHUBB: You're finding me wearisome again.

BLUNT: These painters – Giotto, Piero – they aren't so many failed Raphaels, Leonardos without the know-how. Try to look at them as contemporaries did, judge them on their own terms, not as prefiguring some (to them) unknown future. They didn't know Raphael was going to do it better.

CHUBB: To be quite honest I haven't got to Raphael. But where have I heard that argument before?

BLUNT: If you were planning on going to the British Museum, how was it you remembered to bring the photographs?

CHUBB: I know. It's exactly the same argument you were using to explain what you did in the thirties: it seemed the right thing to do at the time. Giotto didn't have a grasp on perspective and neither did you. The difference being, of course, that art has no consequences.

BLUNT: How did you remember the photographs?

CHUBB: I didn't. I nipped up to the office for them. Good try, though. (*He switches on the screen and the photographs start again.*)

BLUNT: No.

(*Photo.*)

No.

(Titian and a Venetian Senator *now comes up on the screen as we saw it in the opening scene with two figures. The* RESTORER *stands right of the screen as before.*)

RESTORER: This was before cleaning. (*He punches up a slide of the picture after cleaning, now with a third figure (Figure 2).*) This is after cleaning.

BLUNT: I thought there must be something there. With just the two of them, it didn't make sense as a composition.

RESTORER: Quite. Though it doesn't make a lot of sense as a composition now.

BLUNT: No?

RESTORER: Look at Titian. The scale is all wrong. He looks as if he belongs in a different picture.

BLUNT: He does, of course. It's a copy.

RESTORER: Yes.

BLUNT: From the Berlin self-portrait.

RESTORER: Yes.

BLUNT: But at least we know who he is. And who the Chancellor is. But who is the new man? An X-ray, do you think?

RESTORER: Can't do any harm.

BLUNT: Wish it were a better picture. Got the velvet rather well.
(*The* RESTORER *disappears as a photograph of more young men comes up on the screen.*)

CHUBB: And who is the other figure?

BLUNT: I don't know.

CHUBB: You've identified him before in a different context.

BLUNT: So why are you asking me again?

CHUBB: It's the context we're interested in.
(*Photograph.*)
Who's this?

BLUNT: His name was Baker. He was at Oxford. Balliol, possibly.

CHUBB: Handsome.

BLUNT: Is he?

CHUBB: Isn't he?

BLUNT: Dead, anyway.

CHUBB: Naturally. When was that?

BLUNT: The death?

CHUBB: The photograph.

BLUNT: August Bank Holiday, 1935. Margate.

CHUBB: Vanished world. Hooligans on scooters nowadays.
　　(*Photograph.*)
　　Who are these gentlemen?

BLUNT: Chums of Burgess. Cameron Highlanders, I think.
　　Kilted jobs anyway.

CHUBB: Two in a row. Progress.

BLUNT: Not really. I don't suppose they had access to any
　　information above latrine roster level.

CHUBB: They probably had other qualities.

BLUNT: I once had a photograph of Burgess with his head under
　　one of their kilts.
　　(*Photograph.*)

CHUBB: This one?
　　(*Pause.*)

BLUNT: Yes.

CHUBB: Odd, isn't it, that it's the irrelevant details that you can
　　recall. An August Bank Holiday in Margate. Not Worthing.
　　Not the Seaforth Highlanders but the Camerons. (CHUBB
　　drops several slides on the floor. He picks them up.) Facts, faces,
　　you might be expected to remember you forget.

BLUNT: That's the way with memory. The canvas is vague. The
　　details stand out.

CHUBB: It could get tiresome.
　　(*Photograph.*)

BLUNT: No.
　　(*Photograph.*)
　　No.
　　(*A slide of Titian's* Allegory of Prudence *has come up on the
　　screen, in colour* (*Figure 3*).)
　　N – Oh yes.

CHUBB: Sorry. Must have picked up one of yours.

BLUNT: No. Leave it. At least I can tell you their names. But

perhaps you know it. It's in the National Gallery. How far
have you got on your safari through the nation's
masterpieces? Have you reached Titian?

CHUBB: Don't tell me. Venetian. Sixteenth century. A
contemporary of Tintoretto and Veronese. In some sense the
founder of modern painting.

BLUNT: In what sense?

CHUBB: Well, in the sense that he painted character.

BLUNT: Mmm, though it's not the slightest use knowing that
unless you recognize one of his pictures when you see one.

CHUBB: Is this typical?

BLUNT: Actually, no.

CHUBB: Ah.

BLUNT: Though it is Titian at the top of his form. Done towards
the end of his life . . .

CHUBB: Didn't he live until he was ninety-nine?

BLUNT: That has been disputed. What cannot be disputed is the
style, shining with all the autumnal magnificence of his
ultima maniera.

CHUBB: Too plush for me, Titian. All fur and fabric. Don't like
the look of that dog.

BLUNT: That's because that dog is a wolf. (*He points to a creature
on the right.*) That dog is a dog.

CHUBB: Still wouldn't want to be the postman. Who are they all?

BLUNT: The old man on the left is Titian himself.

CHUBB: He *looks* ninety-nine.

BLUNT: . . . The middle-aged man in the centre is Titian's son,
and the young man on the right is probably his adopted
grandson.

CHUBB: I don't care for it, quite honestly.

BLUNT: Oh.

CHUBB: Something of the three wise monkeys about it.

BLUNT: That's not an altogether foolish remark.

CHUBB: Good for Chubb. Why?

BLUNT: Because it's an emblematic painting, a puzzle picture. A
visual paraphrase of the *Three Ages of Man*, obviously, but
something else besides. The clue is the animals.

CHUBB: Was he fond of animals?

BLUNT: Titian? I've no idea. Shouldn't think so for a moment. People weren't.

CHUBB: Rembrandt was. Rembrandt liked dogs.

BLUNT: Rembrandt's dogs, Titian's age. I can see you've been down at the Purley Public Library again. Except that Rembrandt's dogs are different. Rembrandt's dogs tend to be just dogs. This dog is hardly a dog at all.

CHUBB: You mean it's a symbol of fidelity?

BLUNT: It can be.

CHUBB: Hence Fido. And the wolf is a symbol of gluttony.

BLUNT: One hopes the security of the nation is not being neglected in favour of your studies in iconography.

CHUBB: One picks it up, you know.

BLUNT: (Sharply) Well, if you do 'pick it up', pick it up properly. Yes, a dog is a symbol of fidelity and a wolf of gluttony, but occurring together as they do here, in conjunction with the lion, they are disparate parts of a three-headed beast which from classical times onwards has been a symbol of prudence. Hence the title of the picture: the *Allegory of Prudence*.

CHUBB: And I thought I was getting the hang of it.

BLUNT: There isn't a 'hang of it'. There isn't a kit. A wolf can mean gluttony, a dog fidelity, and treachery a cat. But not always. Not automatically. Take the owl. It can be a bird of wisdom, but since it is a bird of the night it can represent the opposite, ignorance and wilful blindness. Hardest of all to accept, it can be just an owl. Of course, one shouldn't blame you. You're just carrying over the techniques of facile identification favoured in your profession, into mine . . . where it isn't quite like that. Appearances deceive. Art is seldom quite what it seems.

CHUBB: Back to the drawing-board. Perhaps we should do some more.

BLUNT: Art?

CHUBB: Facile identification.

BLUNT: No.

(*Photograph.*)

41

No.

(*Photograph.*)

No. Actually, that face does ring a bell.

CHUBB: Yes? (*He goes back to the last photograph.*)

BLUNT: I've seen it.

CHUBB: Who is he?

BLUNT: I told you. Titian's son.

CHUBB: I thought for one delirious moment we were about to make progress.

BLUNT: Where is it? Come along, come along. This is how you learn.

(CHUBB *goes back through the photographs until he reaches the Titian again.*)

I have seen him. Where?

(*A knock at the door.* PHILLIPS, *a student, stands silhouetted in the doorway.*)

PHILLIPS: It's Phillips, sir.

BLUNT: I shan't keep you a moment. I have to teach now. Since Mr Phillips is paying for his time I think he has priority. Perhaps you might wait outside, Phillips, we haven't quite finished.

CHUBB: We haven't even started.

(PHILLIPS *exits.* CHUBB *gathers up the photographs and puts them in his briefcase.*)

I'm not good at cracking the whip. I enjoy our talks.

BLUNT: (*Consulting a reference book*) So you keep saying.

CHUBB: Eyebrows are beginning to be raised. The phrase 'stringing you along' has been mentioned. The feeling is, you see, that you may just be the baby thrown out of the sleigh to slow down the wolves.

BLUNT: And who are these wolves?

CHUBB: They're like this one (*in the Titian*). They look back. They're the ones with hindsight. You've told us some names. You've not told us the names behind the names.

BLUNT: Can I ask you something? Who else knows?

CHUBB: Do you mean, down the road? Somebody had to be told. You were promised immunity, not anonymity. What do you

42

think of the Wallace Collection? Should I go there?

BLUNT: Their Poussin apart, it's a bit chocolate box.

CHUBB: They have the *Laughing Cavalier*.

BLUNT: Exactly. Come in, Phillips.

(CHUBB *leaves as* PHILLIPS *comes in*.)

PHILLIPS: I've seen him once or twice. He comes into the library.

BLUNT: Yes. He's a mature student.

PHILLIPS: I'd say he was a policeman.

BLUNT: Do you have a suit?

PHILLIPS: Suit?

BLUNT: Jacket, trousers, preferably matching. Even, by some sartorial miracle, a waistcoat.

PHILLIPS: I do, as a matter of fact.

BLUNT: And is it handy, or is it in Thornton Heath?

PHILLIPS: I think I can put my hands on it without too much trouble.

BLUNT: Well, go away and put your hands on it and your legs into it and telephone me here at two o'clock.

PHILLIPS: Why, what's happening?

BLUNT: Nothing. A little extra-mural work. Off you go.

(PHILLIPS *goes as the lights fade.* BLUNT *turns to gaze at the* Allegory of Prudence *then switches off the projector as the scene changes*.)

BLUNT's *room recedes, a red carpet runs the breadth of the stage, gilt console tables appear and an elaborate banquette, set against a wall covered in (not over-exciting) paintings. We are in a corridor of Buckingham Palace and prominent among the paintings hanging on the wall is the* Triple Portrait (*Figure 2*).

COLIN, *a young footman in an apron, comes on carrying a picture. He puts the picture down as* PHILLIPS, *now in a suit, follows him carrying a step-ladder and looking wonderingly at the pictures and the furniture*.

COLIN: Jumble. Bric-à-brac.

PHILLIPS: This is a Raphael.

COLIN: The regal equivalent of the fish-slice or the chromium cake-stand. A downstairs attic, this corridor. (*Pause*.) And

43

it's not Raphael. It's school of.

PHILLIPS: How would you know?

COLIN: Because I dust it.

(PHILLIPS *keeps looking up and down the corridor*.)

Nobody's coming. Sir is out practising with his horse and cart, and madam is opening a swimming-bath. Though in the unlikely event anyone does come by, disappear. They are happier thinking the place runs itself.

(PHILLIPS *is looking at an ornate clock*.)

Like that, do you?

PHILLIPS: Liking doesn't necessarily come into it.

COLIN: It's ormolu. I've always had a soft spot for ormolu. Childhood, I suppose. Omolu's fairly thin on the ground in Bethnal Green.

(PHILLIPS *is now looking at a painting*.)

PHILLIPS: Some of these are in terrible condition.

COLIN: I can't think why. They get a wipe over with a damp cloth quite regularly.

PHILLIPS: How did you come to work here?

COLIN: It was either this or the police force. I had the qualifications. Presentable. Good-looking in a standard sort of way. I might even be thought to be public school until I opened my mouth. But of course you don't open your mouth. That's one of the conditions of employment. So are you top boy?

(BLUNT *has come on, unseen by* PHILLIPS.)

PHILLIPS: What?

COLIN: Earned yourself a trip to the Palace, you must have something.

BLUNT: He does. A suit.

Fool of a policeman on the gate. Insisted on going through my briefcase. He said, 'Do you have anything explosive?' I said, 'Yes, I certainly do. An article for the *Burlington Magazine* on Sebastiano del Piombo that is going to blow the place sky-high.' Not amused. I've been walking through that gate for ten years.

How are you today, Colin?

COLIN: Perfectly all right, thank you.

(BLUNT *looks at the* Triple Portrait.)

BLUNT: We're going to take these gentlemen down and put this in its place. This, (*He hands the replacement picture to* PHILLIPS.) as you can see, is an *Annunciation*. Perhaps, Phillips, you could give us a technical description of the panel.

PHILLIPS: Well, it's constructed of two planks, joined by a horizontal brace . . .

BLUNT: Two planks of what?

PHILLIPS: Wood.

BLUNT: Oak? Ash? Chipboard?

PHILLIPS: It's probably poplar.

BLUNT: Why?

PHILLIPS: Because it generally is. (*He turns it over.*)

BLUNT: So that's the back finished, is it? What about the frame?

PHILLIPS: Gilt.

BLUNT: Old gilt or modern gilt?

PHILLIPS: I can't tell.

BLUNT: Colin, any thoughts?

COLIN: Modern, I'd have said. Relatively, anyway. Glazing generally well-preserved. Some worm but there seems to be very little re-touching. Number of holes have been repaired, particularly round knots in the wood. It *is* poplar, actually. Some re-touching here, see. Minute flaking along the outline of the angel's robe. A few *pentimenti* visible to the naked eye, most clearly the fingers of the Virgin's left hand. Reserve judgement on the attribution, but a preliminary impression would suggest Sienna.

BLUNT: Good. Phillips, the steps. Colin, would you move the banquette.

(BLUNT *looks fixedly at the* Triple Portrait *on the wall*.)

Hold the steps. (*He ascends the steps.*) This painting was in the collection of Charles I where it was ascribed to Titian, and it hung with other, rather more plausible, Titians in the palace at Whitehall.

(BLUNT *is addressing this speech to the painting while examining it closely. Meanwhile* COLIN *spots Someone approaching off-stage right. He nudges* PHILLIPS, *indicating he should go.*)

COLIN: Sir.

BLUNT: Shut up. It was sold off after Charles I's execution but was recovered by Charles II and hung quite happily in the royal collection, nobody having any doubts about it at all until the end of the nineteenth century. Titian's beard is so badly done it looks as if it hooks on behind the ears.

(COLIN *and* PHILLIPS *hurriedly scarper, stage left. The stage is empty for a moment or two as* BLUNT *goes on talking to the picture.*)

One lesson to be learned from paintings as indifferent as this, is that there is no such thing as a royal collection. It is rather a royal accumulation.

(HMQ *has entered, quite slowly. She looks. She is about to pass on.*)

Could you hand me my glass. (BLUNT *puts his hand down without looking.*) It's on the table. Come along – we haven't got all day.

(HMQ *thinks twice but then hands him his glass.*)

Thank you. I thought so. Where are my notes? (*He comes down, still with his back to* HMQ.) You're supposed to be holding the steps. I could have fallen flat on my face.

HMQ: I think you already have.

BLUNT: Your Majesty, I'm so sorry.

HMQ: Not at all. One was most instructed. You were about to make a note.

BLUNT: It can wait, Ma'am.

HMQ: No. Carry on, do it now. Ignore me.

BLUNT: Very well, Ma'am.

(HMQ *looks at the picture while* BLUNT *scribbles a note.*)

HMQ: And how did we accumulate this particular picture?

BLUNT: It belonged to Charles I, Ma'am.

HMQ: King Charles I?

BLUNT: Ma'am. It was thought to be by Titian.

HMQ: And now it isn't?

BLUNT: Not altogether, Ma'am.

46

HMQ: I suppose that is part of your function, Sir Anthony, to prove that my pictures are fakes?

BLUNT: Because something is not what it is said to be, Ma'am, does not mean it is a fake. It may just have been wrongly attributed.

HMQ: Yes. It's a fine face, though he looks as if he could do with some fresh air. Who is he?

BLUNT: His name is Andrea Franceschi. He was Chancellor of Venice.

HMQ: We were in Venice two years ago. Unusual place. So. Now that it's a fake, what are you planning to do with it? Put it out for the binmen?

BLUNT: A painting is a document, Ma'am. It has to be read in the context of art history.

HMQ: Has art always had a history? It's all the thing now, isn't it, but one doesn't remember it when one was young. There was art appreciation.

BLUNT: Art history is a part of art appreciation, Ma'am. We know that in this painting the old man is Titian himself; it's copied from one of his self-portraits. That's the Chancellor of Venice, but this other gentleman is something of a mystery. I'm trying to identify him, and with your permission, Ma'am, I'd like to remove the painting to examine it at my leisure.

HMQ: Remove it? I'm not sure I want that. It would leave us with a horrid hole.

BLUNT: I have something to put in its place, Ma'am. (*Indicating the* Annunciation.) It's an *Annunciation*.

HMQ: Yes, I know what it is.

BLUNT: You're not attached to this particular picture, are you, Ma'am?

HMQ: No, but it's there, you know. One's used to it.

BLUNT: I think it was Gertrude Stein who said that after a while even the best pictures turn into wallpaper.

HMQ: Really? This wallpaper is pure silk. I was shown some silkworms once in Sri Lanka. It's their cocoons, you know.

BLUNT: Yes. I had understood you weren't going to be here this afternoon.

HMQ: Obviously. I had understood I wasn't going to be here,

either. I was due to open a swimming bath. Completed on Friday, filled on Saturday, it cracked on Sunday and today it's as dry as a bone. So this afternoon one is, to some extent, kicking one's heels.

BLUNT: That must make a nice change.

HMQ: Not altogether. One likes to know in advance what one is going to be doing, even if one is going to be hanging about. If I am doing nothing, I like to be doing nothing to some purpose. That is what leisure means. (*She indicates an object on a table.*) This ostrich egg was given us by the people of Samoa. It hasn't quite found its place yet. Titian.

BLUNT: Ma'am?

HMQ: That isn't really your period, is it?

BLUNT: In what way?

HMQ: You are an expert on Poussin, are you not?

BLUNT: That's right, Ma'am.

HMQ: Chicken.

BLUNT: Ma'am?

HMQ: Poussin. French for chicken. One has just had it for lunch. I suppose it's fresh in the mind. It was one of what I call my All Walks of Life luncheons. Today we had the head of the CBI, an Olympic swimmer, a primary school headmistress, a General in the Salvation Army, and Glenda Jackson. It was a bit sticky.

BLUNT: I've been to one, Ma'am. That was a bit sticky, too.

HMQ: The trouble is, whenever I meet anybody they're always on their best behaviour. And when one is on one's best behaviour one isn't always at one's best. I don't understand it. They all have different jobs, there ought to be heaps to talk about, yet I'm always having to crank it up.

BLUNT: The truth is, Ma'am, one doesn't have much to say to people very different from oneself. If you'd had the General in the Salvation Army, the Archbishop of Canterbury and the President of the Methodist Conference, they could all have talked about God, and lunch would have been a howling success.

HMQ: Yes. And guess who would have been staring at her plate.

48

And think if they were all actors.

BLUNT: At least they would talk, Ma'am.

HMQ: Correction, Sir Anthony. They wouldn't talk. They would chat. One doesn't want chat. I don't like chat.

BLUNT: Weren't we chatting about Poussin?

HMQ: Were we? Well, we mustn't. We must do it properly. Feed me facts, Sir Anthony. I like a fact. What were his dates?

BLUNT: 1595 to 1665.

HMQ: Seventy. A good age for those days. How many pictures did he do?

BLUNT: Er . . .

HMQ: Don't you know?

BLUNT: I've never been asked that question before, Ma'am. He wasn't a prolific artist.

HMQ: Have we got any?

BLUNT: Paintings, no, Ma'am, but what you do have is a priceless collection of drawings.

HMQ: Oh dear. So many of my things are priceless. Doubly so, really. Priceless because one can't put a price on them, and then if one did one wouldn't be allowed to sell them. Do you have pictures?

BLUNT: One or two, Ma'am.

HMQ: Are they valuable?

BLUNT: Yes, but they are not invaluable. Though I do have a Poussin.

HMQ: You mean you have one and we don't? Something wrong there.

BLUNT: Do you take any pleasure in acquisition, Ma'am?

HMQ: Why? I'm not asking you to make me a present of it. That was one of my grandmother's tricks, Queen Mary. Acquired no end of stuff. Accumulated it. But pleasure in buying things? No. I like buying horses, as everybody knows, but why not? I know about them. But you're right. One more Fabergé egg isn't going to make my day. Go on with your work. Don't let me stop you.

BLUNT: It seems rude.

HMQ: I'm used to it. My days are spent watching people work.

49

My work is watching people work.

BLUNT: Very well, Ma'am. (*He goes on making notes.*)

HMQ: What is it you want to know about the painting?

BLUNT: Many things. It's a problem picture.

HMQ: Not to me. But then I don't suppose wallpaper can be a problem, can it? Where will you take it?

BLUNT: The laboratory.

HMQ: Oh dear. I don't know. But I'm inclined to say no. It's the constant *va et vient* of one's things. A monarch has been defined as someone who doesn't have to look round before sitting down. No longer. One has to look round nowadays because the odds are the Chippendale is on exhibition. (*She picks up a bowl.*) This rose bowl was a wedding present from the people of Jersey.

BLUNT: Do you still have all your wedding presents, Ma'am?

HMQ: Not all. For instance, it was 1947. Clothes were still rationed. Result was, one was inundated with nylons. I don't still have them. Do you like it?

BLUNT: Not altogether, Ma'am.

HMQ: I do, quite. But then I've never set much store by taste. That, after all, is your job. In mine, taste isn't such a good idea. When one looks at my predecessors the monarchs with the best taste . . . I'm thinking of Charles I and George III and IV . . . made a terrible hash of the rest of it. I don't think taste helps. Do you paint?

BLUNT: I'm afraid not, Ma'am. I have no skill in that department.

HMQ: Nor me. The Prince of Wales paints, and my husband. They both claim it is very soothing. As a child I found it the reverse. My colours always used to run. I like things to have a line round them.

BLUNT: You must have had more experience of painters than most.

HMQ: In what way?

BLUNT: Through having your portrait painted.

HMQ: Oh, that. Yes. Though one gets the impression that as artists portrait painters don't really count. Not nowadays anyway.

BLUNT: They're seldom standard-bearers of the avant-garde, Ma'am.

HMQ: They would hardly be painting me if they were. One doesn't
want two noses. Mind you, that would make one no more
unrecognizable than some of their efforts. No resemblance at
all. Sometimes I think it would be simpler to send round to
Scotland Yard for an Identikit. Still I can understand it when
they get me wrong, but some of them get the horse wrong too.
That's unforgivable.

BLUNT: It's true none of them quite capture you.

HMQ: I hope not. I don't think one wants to be captured, does one?
Not entirely, anyway.

BLUNT: You sound like one of those primitive tribes who believe
an image confers some power on the possessor.

HMQ: If I believed that, Sir Anthony, I am in the pocket of anyone
with a handful of change.

BLUNT: Portrait painters tend to regard faces as not very still lives.
There was one eminent portrait painter who said he wished he
could hang his sitters upside down by the leg like a dead hare.

HMQ: Yes. Well, one Minister of the Arts wanted to loose Francis
Bacon on me, and that's probably how I would have ended up.
He did the Screaming Pope, didn't he? I suppose I would have
been the Screaming Queen.
(*He laughs. She doesn't. She picks up something else.*)
This is charming, isn't it. It's antelope horn. A gift from the
National Association of Girls' and Mixed Clubs. Nowadays,
of course, they don't even do sketches; they take photographs,
then take them home and copy them. I think that's cheating.

BLUNT: I'm sure Michelangelo would have used the camera,
Ma'am, if it had been invented. And Leonardo would
probably have invented it.
(*He laughs, but she doesn't.*)

HMQ: You see, I would call doing it from a photograph, *tracing*.
Art, to my mind, has to be what we used to call freehand
drawing. If you paint it from a photograph one might as well
have a photograph.

BLUNT: The portrait everybody likes best does look like a
photograph.

HMQ: The Annigoni. I like that one too. Portraits are supposed to be frightfully self-revealing, aren't they, good ones. Show what one's really like. The secret self. Either that, or the eyes are supposed to follow you round the room. I don't know that one has a secret self. Though it's generally assumed that one has. If it could be proved that one hadn't, some of the newspapers would have precious little to write about. Have you had your portrait painted?

BLUNT: No, Ma'am.

HMQ: So we don't know whether you have a secret self.

BLUNT: I think the only person who doesn't have a secret self, Ma'am, must be God.

HMQ: Oh? How is that?

BLUNT: There is no sense in which one could ask, 'What is God really like?' Never off duty – he must always be the same. It must make it very dull. There can be no gossip in Heaven.

HMQ: Good. I don't like gossip. This clock shows the time not only here but also in Perth, Western Australia. In certain circumstances it could be quite handy. I suppose for me Heaven is likely to be a bit of a comedown. What about you?

BLUNT: I'm not sure I'll get in, Ma'am.

HMQ: Why on earth not? You've done nothing wrong. Your father was a clergyman, after all. Are all owners co-operative about lending their pictures?

BLUNT: None as co-operative as yourself, Ma'am.

HMQ: That is the kind of remark, Sir Anthony, were it in a play, to which one would reply 'Tush!'

BLUNT: Truly, Ma'am.

HMQ: Well, I think I'm going to blot my copybook on this one and persuade you to take St Sebastian instead.

BLUNT: He wouldn't be much use to me, Ma'am.

HMQ: Not much use to anybody. I find him faintly ludicrous. Turned into a human pincushion, and he just looks as if it were a minor inconvenience.

BLUNT: The saints tended to be like that, Ma'am. Though there's more excuse for St Sebastian as he didn't actually die of his wounds.

HMQ: Oh. That was lucky.

BLUNT: He survived and was flogged to death.

HMQ: Oh dear. Out of the frying-pan into the fire. And what about this *Annunciation* you want to foist on to me? Where's it been? In the cellar?

BLUNT: Hampton Court.

HMQ: Same thing. What should I know about the *Annunciation*? Come along. Facts.

BLUNT: The Virgin is traditionally discovered reading. It's quite amusing that as time went on painters tended to elevate the status of the Holy Family, so that Joseph, from being a simple carpenter, eventually comes to be depicted as a full-blown architect; and the Virgin, who to begin with is just given a book, ends up with a reading desk and a whole library, so that in some later versions Gabriel looks as if he is delivering his message to the Mistress of Girton.

(He laughs. She doesn't.)

HMQ: Girton, Cambridge?

BLUNT: Yes, Ma'am.

HMQ: I opened them a new kitchen. Their gas cookers are among the most advanced in East Anglia. You see, one reason why I prefer that to this is that in a home (and this is a home, albeit only one of one's homes) one doesn't want too many pictures of what I would call a religious flavour. I mean, this isn't a church. Besides, this (*the* Triple Portrait) I think is rather unusual, whereas *Annunciation*s are quite common. When we visited Florence we were taken round the art gallery there, and there – well, I won't say *Annunciation*s are two a penny, but they certainly were quite thick on the ground. And not all of them very convincing. My husband remarked that one of them looked to him like the messenger arriving from Littlewoods Pools. And that the Virgin was protesting she had put a cross for no publicity. Fortunately, Signor de Gasperi's English was not good, or we should have had the Pope on our tracks. (HMQ *picks up an object.*) Do you know what this is made out of? Coal. Given us by the Welsh miners. How long would you want it for, my Titian? My fake Titian.

BLUNT: A few weeks.

HMQ: Oh, very well. You see, what I don't like is the assumption that one doesn't notice, one doesn't care. Still, we're off to Zambia next week, so that will cushion the blow. One never stops, you know. Governments come and go. Or don't go. One never stops. Could I ask you a question, Sir Anthony? Have I many forgeries? What about these?

BLUNT: Paintings of this date are seldom forgeries, Ma'am. They are sometimes not what we think they are, but that's different. The question doesn't pose itself in the form, 'Is this a fake?' so much as 'Who painted this picture and why?' Is it Titian, or a pupil or pupils of Titian? Is it someone who paints like Titian because he admires him and can't help painting in the same way? The public are rather tiresomely fascinated by forgery – more so, I'm afraid, than they are by the real thing.

HMQ: Yes, well, as a member in this instance (somewhat unusually for me) of the public, I also find a forgery fascinating.

BLUNT: Paintings make no claims, Ma'am. They do not purport to be anything other than paintings. It is we, the beholders, who make claims for them, attribute a picture to this artist or that.

HMQ: With respect, Sir Anthony, rubbish. What if a painting is signed and the signature is a forgery?

BLUNT: Forgery of that kind is much more a feature of modern or relatively modern paintings than of Old Masters, Ma'am.

HMQ: Again, Sir Anthony, I find myself having to disagree with you. We were in Holland not long ago and after we had been taken to see the tulips and a soil structure laboratory, Queen Juliana showed us her Vermeers. One has a Vermeer, so one was quite interested.

BLUNT: I think I know what you are going to say, Ma'am.
(HMQ *gives him a sharp look*.)
. . . but please go ahead and say it.

HMQ: Thank you, and (though you're obviously ahead of me) she showed us some of the forged Vermeers done by a Mr . . .

BLUNT: Van Meegeren.

HMQ: Quite. Those were forgeries. Of Old Masters.

BLUNT: Ma'am is quite right.

HMQ: Moreover, these Van Meegerens didn't seem to me to be
the least bit like. Terrible daubs. God knows, one is no
expert on Vermeer, but if I could tell they were fakes why
couldn't other people see it at the time? When was it, in the
forties?

BLUNT: It's a complicated question, Ma'am.

HMQ: Oh, don't spare me. Remember I could have been opening
a swimming bath.

BLUNT: What has exposed them as forgeries, Ma'am, is not any
improvement in perception, but time. Though a forger
reproduce in the most exact fashion the style and detail of his
subject, as a painter he is nevertheless of his time and
however slavishly he imitates, he does it in the fashion of his
time, in a way that is contemporary, and with the passage of
years it is this element that dates, begins to seem old-
fashioned, and which eventually unmasks him.

HMQ: Interesting. I suppose too the context of the painting
matters. Its history and provenance (is that the word?) confer
on it a certain respectability. This can't be a forgery, it's in
such and such a collection, its background and pedigree are
impeccable – besides, it has been vetted by the experts. Isn't
that how the argument goes? So if one comes across a
painting with the right background and pedigree, Sir
Anthony, then it must be hard, I imagine – even
inconceivable – to think that it is not what it claims to be.
And even supposing someone in such circumstances did have
suspicions, they would be chary about voicing them. Easier
to leave things as they are in every department. Stick to the
official attribution rather than let the cat out of the bag and
say, 'Here we have a fake.'

BLUNT: I still think the word 'fake' is inappropriate, Ma'am.

HMQ: If something is not what it is claimed to be, what is it?

BLUNT: An enigma?

HMQ: That is, I think, the sophisticated answer. It's curious, Sir

55

Anthony, but all the time we have been talking, there has been a young man skulking behind one of my Louis XV *bergères* (a gift from the de Gaulles). Do you think he is waiting to assassinate one, or does he have an interest in that particular *ébéniste*?

BLUNT: My assistant, Ma'am.

HMQ: I think it's time he was flushed from his lair. Come in, hiddy or not, young man.

(PHILLIPS *comes on left.*)

BLUNT: This is Mr Phillips, Ma'am, a student at the Courtauld Institute.

PHILLIPS: Your Majesty.

HMQ: What do you plan to do with your art history?

PHILLIPS: I am hoping to go into one of the big auction houses, Ma'am.

HMQ: Jolly good. That should keep you out of mischief. Did you ever consider that, Sir Anthony?

BLUNT: No, Ma'am.

HMQ: Oh. Well, I must be on my way. Not, I think, a wasted afternoon. One has touched upon art, learned a little iconography, and something of fakes and forgery. Facts not chat. Of course, had I been opening the swimming bath I would have picked up one or two facts there: the pumping system; the filter process; the precautions against infectious diseases of the feet. All facts. One never knows when they may come in handy.

Be careful how you go up the ladder, Sir Anthony. One could have a nasty fall.

BLUNT: Ma'am.

HMQ: Mr Phillips. (HMQ *exits left.*)

PHILLIPS: She seems quite on the ball.

BLUNT: Oh, yes.

PHILLIPS: The furniture, the pictures. I thought it was all horses.

(COLIN *enters left.*)

COLIN: What the hell was madam doing here? What happened to the swimming bath?

PHILLIPS: There was a leak.

56

COLIN: I bet that made her shirty. They like their routine.

BLUNT: Strange about the Royal Family. They ask you a great deal but tell you very little.

COLIN: What were you talking about?

BLUNT: I was talking about art. I'm not sure that she was. Come on, let's get this bloody picture down.

(BLUNT *watches as* COLIN *takes down the* Triple Portrait *and replaces it with the* Annunciation. *As* COLIN *carries off the* Triple Portrait *the Palace set disappears and* BLUNT, *pointer in hand, is once more found lecturing at the Courtauld Institute.*)

And should we compare these two paintings it is plain straightaway that they do not compare – at any rate in terms of quality. One, the *Allegory of Prudence*, (*Slide of the* Allegory of Prudence (*Figure 3*)) wholly authentic, Titian at the height of his powers, the other (*Slide of the* Triple Portrait (*Figure 2*)) a hotchpotch, a studio job, Titian's hand possibly to be detected in the striking central figure but nowhere else. But let us leave quality and authenticity aside while I direct your attention to two of the personages depicted in the paintings.

(*A composite slide with Titian's son from the* Allegory of Prudence *on the left and the third man from the* Triple Portrait *on the right (Figure 4).*)

On the left, Titian's son Orazio Vecelli as he appears in the · *Allegory of Prudence*. No doubt about him or his identity and rather a bruiser he looks, like one of those extravagant villains in an early Chaplin film. On the right, altogether more civilized, if not so well painted, is this gentleman.

Younger, perhaps, and with a beard which has not yet achieved its full tropical luxuriance, but with the same eyes, the same nose, surely this is the same man, Titian's son also. The identification has never been made, and I make it now only tentatively and, I hasten to say, to no larger purpose, because even if correct I cannot say it helps to solve the riddle of this picture – if indeed it is a riddle worth solving. But riddle there undoubtedly is as I shall show you. Let us look at the painting as it was when it first turns up in the collection of Charles I some three hundred and fifty years ago. Catalogued as *Titian and a Venetian Senator*, you will note that it then contained only two figures.

(*Slide of the* Triple Portrait *before cleaning* (*Figure 1*).)

When I was appointed Surveyor of the Queen's Pictures, I had the painting cleaned, and the presence of the mysterious gentleman on the right was revealed.

(*Slide of the* Triple Portrait *after cleaning* (*Figure 2*).)

So, having started with two men, we now have a third man. And that is how the picture looks at the moment. But that is only how it looks. Because in addition to being cleaned, I also had the picture X-rayed. And the X-ray revealed a fourth man.

(*Slide of an X-ray photograph of the* Triple Portrait.*)

And that was not the end of it either, for if we rotate the X-ray we find behind the original pair and the third and fourth man the rather more substantial figure of a fifth man.

(*Slide of the X-ray rotated.*)

The fifth man, you will doubtless be relieved to learn, is the last of the sitters lurking in this somewhat over-populated canvas. Who all these figures are and who painted them we do not know. It may be that the third man is indeed Titian's son, but even so that does not help us identify the fourth man or the fifth. And why, you're entitled to ask, does it matter? This is not an important picture, just a murky corner of sixteenth-century art history that wants clearing up but won't be. It matters, I suggest to you as a warning.

(*Slide of the* Triple Portrait (*Figure 2*).)

This painting is a riddle, and this and similar riddles are quests one can pursue for years; their solution is one of the functions of the art historian. But it is only *one* of his functions. Art history is seldom thought of as a hazardous profession. But a life spent teasing out riddles of this kind carries its own risks . . . a barrenness of outlook, a pedantry

* As reproduced in the *Burlington Magazine*, vol. 100, 1958.

that verges on the obsessive, and a farewell to common sense; the rule of the hobby horse. Because, though the solution might add to our appreciation of this painting, paintings, we must never forget, are not there primarily to be solved. A great painting will still elude us, as art will always elude exposition. (*The transition from lecture hall to* BLUNT's *room begins as the light grows on* CHUBB, *in raincoat. He picks up a paper from* BLUNT's *desk and reads it.*)

CHUBB: A long time ago when I first started, I thought . . . or thought that I thought . . . that art was in the front line. I used to review then. I was the art critic of *The Spectator* . . . and I sang the praises of realism from Rembrandt to Rivera, deplored Picasso and abstraction . . . inaccessible to the people, I suppose. What none of us, I suppose, realized then was that the people would mean the public to the extent it does today. (BLUNT *enters. He is in full evening dress with the ribbons and medals of his various orders and decorations. He carries a bottle of whisky and two glasses.*)
What's this?

BLUNT: My speech. The Academy Dinner.

CHUBB: I hadn't planned on calling. I saw your light was on.

BLUNT: Yes. I suppose it's what you'd call a function.

CHUBB: Who was there?

BLUNT: Oh, everybody. Including your boss. We chatted. Do you not get invited to occasions like that?

CHUBB: No.

BLUNT: You should.

CHUBB: I'd feel a bit lost.

BLUNT: Oh, I don't think so. They were all there.

CHUBB: Who?

BLUNT: The great and the good. Everybody on your list. Your little list.

CHUBB: Anyway, I don't have the clothes.

BLUNT: Clothes are the least of it. Your wife would like it. Plenty to goggle at. And in the absence of the public one can see the art. Drink?

CHUBB: Thank you. I came to give you a warning. There is a time coming, soon, when your anonymity will cease to be in any practical sense useful.

BLUNT: Yes, yes, yes.

CHUBB: You must understand that your situation does not improve with time. More and more questions are being asked. The wolves, if you like, are getting closer. We may have to throw you off our sledge now. The consequences will be embarrassing, and not only for you. For us too. It will be painful. You will be the object of scrutiny, explanations sought after, your history gone into. You will be named. Attributed.

BLUNT: And as a fake I shall, of course, excite more interest than the genuine article.

CHUBB: There is someone else. Someone behind you all. All the evidence points to it.

BLUNT: The evidence! Once upon a time, when Berenson began his pioneer work of listing and attributing the paintings of the Italian Renaissance, he would sometimes come across groups of works in which he detected a family resemblance. They pointed to the existence of artists to whom he could not give a name. And there was one, a group of drawings, that resembled – but were not – the work of Botticelli. So he called the putative author of these drawings Amico di Sandro – the friend of Botticelli. But as the work of attribution progressed, Berenson came to see that these drawings were actually the early work of the Florentine painter, Filippino Lippi. There was no Amico di Sandro. He had been invented to fit the evidence, but he did not exist.

CHUBB: It's funny you should mention Berenson. I've just got on to him. Fascinating chap. Only wasn't there another group of paintings he was puzzled about? Of the Mother and Child? Same situation, they resembled one another in style but he couldn't put a name to the artist. The one element they all had in common was that the Christ child wasn't portrayed as the usual torpid, overweight infant but as a real, live wriggling baby. So this process of attribution called into being a painter Berenson called the Maestro del Bambino

Vispo . . . the painter of the wriggling baby. I've not got very far in my studies in art history, of course, and you'll correct me if I'm wrong, but that attribution . . . the Maestro del Bambino Vispo still stands. He did exist.

BLUNT: Yes. That's right. He did. But whether your man existed, or still exists, is a different matter. But very good. You might have made an art historian.

CHUBB: Yes? Did I miss my way?

BLUNT: Not really. Both our professions carry the same risks, after all . . . a barrenness of outlook, a pedantry that verges on the obsessive, a farewell to commonsense, the rule of the hobby horse. You with your hobby horse, me with mine. (CHUBB *punches up the X-ray of the fifth man.*)

CHUBB: Who are they all?

BLUNT: Oh no, not more photographs. (*He looks round at the screen.*) I'm sorry. I thought they were yours, not mine. When I was in the security service art used to be a haven, you know. A refuge. In the silly, knowing jargon of the spy story, a safe house. Not so safe now. Everybody's into art.

CHUBB: Including me.

BLUNT: Still, I think it will last my time. But who are they all? (BLUNT *switches the slide off.*) I don't know that it matters. Behind them lurk other presences, other hands. A whole gallery of possibilities. The real Titian an Allegory of Prudence. The false one an Allegory of Supposition. It is never-ending.

(CHUBB *and* BLUNT *sit looking at one another for a long moment before the lights fade.*)